Cats

by Caroline Arnold
photographs by Richard R. Hewett

Lerner Publications Company • Minneapolis, Minnesota

To my two cats, Rocky and Stella
—CA

Thanks to our series consultant, Sharyn Fenwick, elementary science/math specialist. Mrs. Fenwick was the winner of the National Science Teachers Association 1991 Distinguished Teaching Award. She also was the recipient of the Presidential Award for Excellence in Math and Science Teaching, representing the state of Minnesota at the elementary level in 1992.

The photographs on pages 4 and 12 are reproduced through the courtesy of Caroline Arnold.

Early Bird Nature Books were conceptualized by Ruth Berman and designed by Steve Foley. Series editor is Joelle Goldman.

Website address: www.lernerbooks.com

Text copyright © 1999 by Caroline Arnold
Photographs copyright © 1999 by Richard R. Hewett, except where noted

Library of Congress Cataloging-in-Publication Data

Arnold, Caroline.
    Cats / by Caroline Arnold ; photographs by Richard R. Hewett.
       p. cm. — (Early bird nature books)
    Includes index.
    Summary: Describes the physical characteristics, behavior, and life cycle of domestic cats, as well as their place in the cat family.
    ISBN 0-8225-3032-5 (alk. paper)
    1. Cats—Juvenile literature. 2. Felidae—Juvenile literature.
[1. Cats.] I. Hewett, Richard, ill. II. Title. III. Series.
SF445.7.A76 1999
636.8—dc21   98-38206

Manufactured in the United States of America
1 2 3 4 5 6 – SP – 04 03 02 01 00 99

Contents

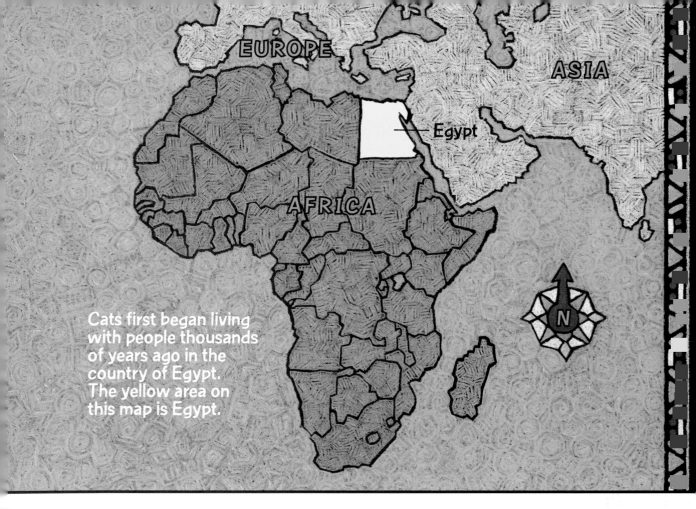

EUROPE

ASIA

Egypt

AFRICA

N

Cats first began living with people thousands of years ago in the country of Egypt. The yellow area on this map is Egypt.

Be a Word Detective

Can you find these words as you read about the cat's life? Be a detective and try to figure out what they mean. You can turn to the glossary on page 46 for help.

breeds   **nocturnal**   **stalking**

carnivores   **predators**   **tapetum lucidum**

domestic   **prey**   **territory**

nest

5

The scientific name for pet cats is Felis domesticus. *What else do we call a pet cat?*

The Cat Family

 Cats are beautiful animals. They have sleek bodies and soft fur. They move gracefully. Cats help people by killing mice and other pests. Cats also are good pets.

The cats that people keep as pets are called domestic (duh-MESS-tihk) cats. There are many breeds of domestic cats. The breeds are different colors, shapes, and sizes. But all breeds of domestic cats are the same species (SPEE-sheez), or kind.

There are about 25 different breeds of domestic cats. This is a Persian cat. Persian cats have long fur.

There are 35 species of cats in the world. They are divided into three groups. The groups are the big cats, the cheetah, and the small cats.

There are six species of cats in the big cat group. They are the lion, tiger, leopard, jaguar, clouded leopard, and snow leopard.

Lions are big cats who live in Africa and Asia.

Cheetahs can run faster than any other animal. They can run 65 miles per hour for short distances.

Cheetahs are large. But they are not in the big cat group. They are in their own group. Cheetahs are very different from other large cats. Cheetahs have bigger chests, longer legs, and slimmer bodies than other large cats. Also, most cats can pull their claws into their paws. Cheetahs are the only cats who cannot do this.

The small cat group includes domestic cats, bobcats, cougars, and many other species. Most of these cats are small or medium-sized, except for the cougar. A cougar can weigh up to 200 pounds!

Bobcats have tufted ears and a short tail. A bobcat is about twice as big as a domestic cat.

People have many different names for the cougar. Puma, panther, and mountain lion are some of these names.

The small cats and the cheetah can purr. The big cats cannot purr nearly as well. But most of the big cats can roar. Small cats and cheetahs cannot roar at all.

Chapter 2

Some domestic cats live indoors. Others live outside. What do we call the place where a cat lives?

A Cat's Neighborhood

Domestic cats usually live alone. Each cat has its own neighborhood. This neighborhood is called a territory. A cat's territory is where it lives. A cat's territory may be as large as a farm. Or it may be as small as one room in a house.

A cat marks the edges of its territory. It marks its territory by scratching or rubbing against objects. Some cats urinate on objects to mark their territory. Scratch marks and urine are like signs. They tell other cats to keep out.

Cats who live in cities usually have smaller territories than cats who live in the country.

Cats check their territories often. They want to make sure everything is all right. That is why house cats go in and out so often. If a cat finds another cat in its territory, the two cats may fight.

Cats who live indoors often want to go outside. Some people have special doors so their pet cats can go in and out on their own.

When a cat is afraid, it arches its back and puffs up its fur. It tries to look bigger than it is. It wants to scare its enemy away.

When cats go out, they must always watch for danger. If a cat meets a dog, the cat may run away. Or it may hiss, arch its back, and puff up its fur to try to scare the dog away. Sometimes a dog comes too close to a cat. Then the cat uses its sharp claws to scratch the dog's nose.

Chapter 3

Cats are good hunters. What do we call animals who hunt other animals?

Expert Hunters

 Cats are meat eaters. Animals who eat meat are called carnivores (KAHR-nuh-vorz).

Cats are also predators (PREH-duh-turz).
Predators are animals who hunt other animals.
The animals that a predator hunts are called
its prey (PRAY).

Domestic cats often hunt mice and other small animals.

All cats know how to hunt. Pet cats do not need to hunt for food, because people feed them. But if pet cats go outside, they will still hunt birds and small animals.

Most pet cats do not need to catch their own food.

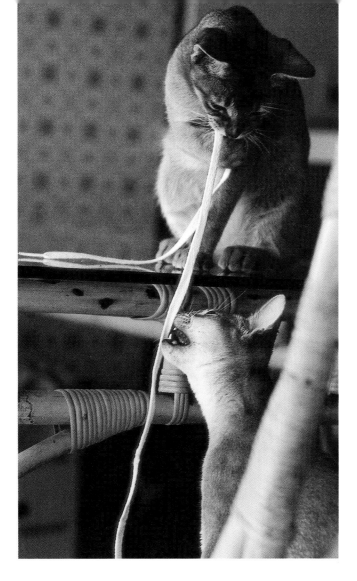

The animals that cats hunt make small, quick movements. Cats like toys that move the same way. These cats are playing with a shoelace.

Many domestic cats live indoors all the time. They never have the chance to hunt prey in the wild. But when they chase a ball or play with string, they act as if they were hunting prey.

Most cats have long tails. A cat's tail helps it keep its balance.

A cat's body is made for hunting. Cats have long legs, narrow bodies, and small heads. They can slip through thick bushes or small openings as they hunt for prey. Most cats can walk easily along narrow ledges and in high places.

Domestic cats are small animals. But they are strong for their size. They have powerful back legs. They use their strong legs to jump and pounce.

A domestic cat can easily jump five times its own length. That's like a human jumping to the roof of a two-story house!

A cat's claws are great for climbing trees. Inset: A cat has four toes on each back paw and five toes on each front paw. Each toe has its own sharp claw.

Cats are good climbers. They can easily go up trees to hunt for prey or to escape from danger. A cat's sharp claws help it to climb. Cats sometimes scratch their claws on trees or other objects. Scratching helps keep their claws needle sharp.

Sometimes cats fall from high places. But they rarely get hurt. They can twist around in the air and land on their feet.

A cat can jump down from a high place without being hurt.

The dark opening at the center of a cat's eye is called the pupil. In bright light, a cat's pupils close to narrow slits (left). *In dim light, they open wide to let in as much light as possible* (right).

Cats have good eyesight. They can see well even in dim light. Many animals that cats hunt are nocturnal (nahk-TUR-nuhl). Nocturnal animals are most active at night. Seeing well at night helps cats find nocturnal prey.

If you see a cat at night, its eyes may seem to shine. They shine because there is a tapetum lucidum (tuh-PEE-tuhm LOO-sih-duhm) at the back of each eye. The tapetum lucidum is shiny. It acts like a mirror. It reflects light into the cat's eye. The tapetum lucidum helps cats see well even when the light is dim.

Cats also hear well. They can find prey by listening. Cats can hear a mouse move in the grass. They can hear a mouse's tiny squeaks.

A cat's whiskers help it feel its way in the dark.

Cats who are hunting often hide in thick bushes or grass. Then they wait for a small animal to come near.

A cat hunts by stalking (STAW-king). It sneaks up to its prey. First, the cat crouches down on the ground. It waits quietly for a bird or small animal to come by. Then the cat creeps forward until it is close to its prey. Finally the cat pounces. It uses its teeth and claws to grab its prey.

Cats have sharp teeth. Their teeth are good for cutting and tearing meat. Cats do not chew meat much. Instead, they bite off chunks and swallow them. Strong juices in their stomach help to break up the chunks of meat.

An adult domestic cat has 30 teeth.

A cat's long tongue can reach up as high as its nose.

A cat has a long tongue. It is covered with tiny spikes. The spikes make the tongue rough like sandpaper. A cat's tongue is good for licking scraps of meat off bones.

A cat can lap up water or milk with its tongue. The cat curls the end and sides of its tongue. Then it scoops the liquid into its mouth.

Like all animals, cats need water to drink. Adult cats do not need to drink milk, but many seem to like it.

A cat also uses its tongue to clean its fur. When a cat licks itself, its rough tongue works like a brush or comb. The tiny spikes smooth the cat's fur.

A cat licks its paws. Then it uses its paws to wash its face and ears.

Domestic cats rest or sleep about 16 hours a day.

If a cat is not patrolling its territory, eating, or cleaning itself, it is probably asleep. Cats are champion sleepers. They can fall asleep at almost any time. They may nap for just a few minutes. Or they may sleep for an hour or more. By resting so much of the time, cats save energy.

Chapter 4

A female cat can have one to eight kittens at a time. Where are her kittens born?

Kittens

 When a female cat is about to have kittens, she picks a quiet, safe place. This place is called her nest. The nest is where her kittens will be born.

A newborn kitten is about 5 inches long and weighs 2 to 4 ounces. These kittens are drinking their mother's milk.

When the kittens are born, the mother cat curls around them to keep them warm. The kittens snuggle up to her belly. They begin to drink her milk.

The eyes of newborn kittens are tightly shut. When the kittens are 8 to 11 days old, their eyes open. Then they can see. A few days later, the kittens begin to crawl around the nest. Soon they are ready to go exploring.

This kitten is 10 days old. Its eyes have just started to open.

These kittens are three weeks old.

Young kittens grow quickly. By the time they are four weeks old, they have started to go farther away from the nest. They play with each other and chase their mother's tail.

These kittens are exploring the area around their nest.

It looks like kittens play just for fun. But playing is exercise for kittens. It also helps them learn about their world.

When kittens are eight weeks old, they have grown teeth. They can eat solid food. They no longer need to drink their mother's milk.

If a kitten gets lost while it is exploring, it meows. Its mother hears the meowing and knows where to find the kitten.

When kittens play, they are practicing hunting.

A mother cat who lives outside teaches her kittens to hunt. A mother cat who stays inside a house does not need to do this. When her kittens can eat solid food, they can leave her. They can go to new homes.

Kittens grow into adult cats in about one year. Then they can start their own families.

Kittens seem to like people as much as people like kittens.

Chapter 5

Cats and people have been friends for a long time. Why did cats start living with people?

Cats and People

 Long ago, there were only wild cats.
No cats lived with people. But many mice and

40

rats lived near people. They ate the food that people had in their homes. Some wild cats learned that they could find prey where people lived. So the cats began to live near people too.

Abyssinian cats are a breed of domestic cats. They look much like the wild cats who first lived near people.

People in long-ago Egypt loved cats. When pet cats died, their owners made them into mummies.

About 6,000 years ago, people in the country of Egypt began to bring cats into their homes. The people wanted the cats to keep mice and rats away from their food. After a while, the cats became tame. They were no longer like their wild relatives. They had become domestic cats. Later, people in other places began to use cats to get rid of pests too.

Domestic cats are one of our best-loved pets. The next time you see a cat, try to imagine a wild cat stalking a mouse long ago in Egypt. That is how we first began living with these small, furry hunters.

Many people keep cats as pets. About 58 million pet cats live in the United States. About 4 million live in Canada.

On Sharing a Book

As you know, adults greatly influence a child's attitude toward reading. When a child sees you read, or when you share a book with a child, you're sending a message that reading is important. Show the child that reading a book together is important to you. Find a comfortable, quiet place. Turn off the television and limit other distractions, such as telephone calls.

Be prepared to start slowly. Take turns reading parts of this book. Stop and talk about what you're reading. Talk about the photographs. You may find that much of the shared time is spent discussing just a few pages. This discussion time is valuable for both of you, so don't move through the book too quickly. If the child begins to lose interest, stop reading. Continue sharing the book at another time. When you do pick up the book again, be sure to revisit the parts you have already read. Most importantly, enjoy the book!

Be a Vocabulary Detective

You will find a word list on page 5. Words selected for this list are important to the understanding of the topic of this book. Encourage the child to be a word detective and search for the words as you read the book together. Talk about what the words mean and how they are used in the sentence. Do any of these words have more than one meaning? You will find these words defined in a glossary on page 46.

What about Questions?

Use questions to make sure the child understands the information in this book. Here are some suggestions:

What did this paragraph tell us? What does this picture show? What do you think we'll learn about next? What kinds of sounds do cats make? How does a domestic cat mark its territory? What does a cat do when an enemy comes near? What do cats eat? How do cats hunt? What does a cat use its tongue for? How many kittens does a mother cat have at one time? How long does it take a kitten to grow into an adult cat? What is your favorite part of the book? Why?

If the child has questions, don't hesitate to respond with questions of your own, such as: What do *you* think? Why? What is it that you don't know? If the child can't remember certain facts, turn to the index.

Introducing the Index

The index is an important learning tool. It helps readers get information quickly without searching throughout the whole book. Turn to the index on page 47. Choose an entry, such as *claws,* and ask the child to use the index to find out how a cat keeps its claws sharp. Repeat this exercise with as many entries as you like. Ask the child to point out the differences between an index and a glossary. (The index helps readers find information quickly, while the glossary tells readers what words mean.)

Where in the World?

Many plants and animals found in the Early Bird Nature Books series live in parts of the world other than the United States. Encourage the child to find the places mentioned in this book on a world map or globe. Take time to talk about climate, terrain, and how you might live in such places.

All the World in Metric!

Although our monetary system is in metric units (based on multiples of 10), the United States is one of the few countries in the world that does not use the metric system of measurement. Here are some conversion activities you and the child can do using a calculator:

WHEN YOU KNOW:	MULTIPLY BY:	TO FIND:
miles	1.609	kilometers
feet	0.3048	meters
inches	2.54	centimeters
gallons	3.787	liters
tons	0.907	metric tons
pounds	0.454	kilograms

Activities

Make up a story about a domestic cat. Be sure to include information from this book. Draw or paint pictures to illustrate your story.

Visit a zoo to see tigers, lions, and other kinds of cats. How are the cats in the zoo similar to domestic cats, and how are they different?

Watch a house cat playing with a toy. Notice how the cat stalks the toy and then pounces on it. What kinds of toys does the cat like best?

Glossary

breeds—types of cats, such as Siamese or Persian. Each breed looks different from other breeds.

carnivores (KAHR-nuh-vorz)—animals who eat flesh or meat

domestic (duh-MESS-tihk)—tamed to live with people

nest—a quiet, safe place where kittens are born

nocturnal (nahk-TUR-nuhl)—active at night

predators (PREH-duh-turz)—animals who hunt other animals

prey (PRAY)—animals who are hunted and eaten by other animals

stalking (STAW-king)—hunting an animal by sneaking up on it

tapetum lucidum (tuh-PEE-tuhm LOO-sih-duhm)—the shiny area at the back of a cat's eye. The tapetum lucidum helps a cat see well when the light is dim.

territory—the area where a cat lives

Index

Pages listed in **bold** type refer to photographs.

About the Author

Caroline Arnold is the author of more than 100 books for young readers. Her well-received Lerner Publishing Group titles include *Bobcats, Cats: In from the Wild, Saving the Peregrine Falcon, A Walk on the Great Barrier Reef,* and *Watching Desert Wildlife.* Since childhood, she has been fascinated with cats, both as pets and in the wild. She grew up in Minneapolis, Minnesota, and studied art at Grinnell College and the University of Iowa. Ms. Arnold lives in Los Angeles, California.

About the Photographer

Richard R. Hewett was born and raised in St. Paul, Minnesota. He graduated from California's Art Center School of Design with a major in photojournalism. He has illustrated more than 50 children's books and collaborated with Caroline Arnold on the Lerner Publishing Group titles *Bobcats, Saving the Peregrine Falcon, Tule Elk,* and *Ostriches and Other Flightless Birds.* Dick and his wife, writer Joan Hewett, live in southern California.

The Early Bird Nature Books Series

African Elephants	Horses	Sandhill Cranes
Alligators	Jellyfish	Scorpions
Ants	Manatees	Sea Lions
Apple Trees	Moose	Sea Turtles
Bobcats	Mountain Goats	Slugs
Brown Bears	Mountain Gorillas	Swans
Cats	Peacocks	Tarantulas
Cockroaches	Penguins	Tigers
Cougars	Polar Bears	Venus Flytraps
Crayfish	Popcorn Plants	Vultures
Dandelions	Prairie Dogs	Walruses
Dolphins	Rats	Whales
Giant Sequoia Trees	Red-Eyed Tree Frogs	White-Tailed Deer
Herons	Saguaro Cactus	Wild Turkeys